W9-CNB-626

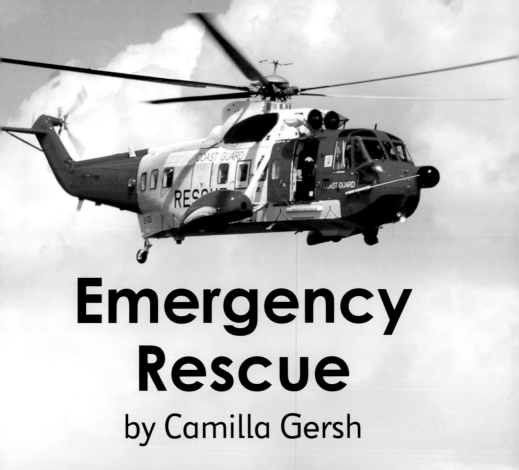

Emergency Rescue

by Camilla Gersh

Series Editor Deborah Lock
Project Editor Caryn Jenner
Editor Nandini Gupta
Designer Charlotte Jennings
Art Editor Yamini Panwar
Senior Art Editor Ann Cannings
US Senior Editor Shannon Beatty

Producer, Pre-production Nadine King
DTP Designers Nand Kishor Acharya,
Dheeraj Singh
Picture Researcher Nishwan Rasool
Managing Editor Soma B. Chowdhury
Managing Art Editor Ahlawat Gunjan
Art Director Martin Wilson

Reading Consultant
Linda Gambrell, Ph.D.

Subject Consultants
Brian Lamm, Firefighter
Jeffrey Lamm, Police Detective

First American Edition 2016
Published in the United States by DK Publishing,
345 Hudson Street, New York, New York 10014

A catalog record for this book is available from the Library of Congress.

ISBN: 978-1-4654-4505-6 (Paperback)
ISBN: 978-1-4654-4500-1 (Hardcover)

Printed and bound in China.

DK books are available at special discounts when purchased in bulk for sales promotions,
premiums, fund-raising, or educational use. For details, contact: DK Publishing Special Markets,
345 Hudson Street, New York, New York 10014 or SpecialSales@dk.com

The publisher would like to thank the following for their kind permission to reproduce their photographs:
(Key: a-above; b-below/bottom; c-center; f-far; l-left; r-right; t-top)
1 Dreamstime.com: Victoria Whitehead. 2 iStockphoto.com: AlexSava (br); franckreporter (bc). 2–3 Dreamstime.com: Mike_kiev (b).
3 Alamy Images: J Orr (tr). Getty Images: Valerie Macon (br). 4 Alamy Images: Hirdes/F1online digitale Bildagentur GmbH (t). Getty Images: Valerie Macon (bc).
4–5 Dreamstime.com: Mike_kiev (b). 5 Alamy Images: Eric Nathan (b). 6 iStockphoto.com: webphotographeer (t). 6–7 Dreamstime.com: Mike_kiev (b).
7 Corbis: Mike Kemp/Rubberball. 8 iStockphoto.com: webphotographeer (t). 8–9 Dreamstime.com: Mike_kiev (b). 9 iStockphoto.com: AlexSava (bl);
webphotographeer (b). 10 Dreamstime.com: Mamuka Gotsiridze (bl). 11 Dreamstime.com: Mamuka Gotsiridze (br). 12 Alamy Images: Hirdes/F1online digitale
Bildagentur GmbH (t). Getty Images: Valerie Macon (bl). 12–13 Dreamstime.com: Darvidanoar; Mike_kiev (b). 14 Getty Images: Valerie Macon (br); Oli Scarff (t).
14–15 Dreamstime.com: Mike_kiev (b). 15 Dreamstime.com: Sandra Van Der Steen (c). 16 iStockphoto.com: anthonysp (t). 16–17 Dreamstime.com: Mike_kiev (b).
17 Getty Images: Valerie Macon (bl). iStockphoto.com: andipantz (c). 18–19 Alamy Images: Keith Dannemiller (t). Dreamstime.com: Mike_kiev (b).
19 Getty Images: Valerie Macon (bc). 20 Alamy Images: Tony Kwan (crb); Sunpix (c). Dreamstime.com: Mamuka Gotsiridze (bl). Getty Images: Jewel Samad/AFP
Photo (clb). 21 Alamy Images: Martyn Goddard (cl); Markus Keller/imageBROKER (cr); Nik Taylor (clb). Dreamstime.com: Mamuka Gotsiridze (br).
22 Dreamstime.com: Mamuka Gotsiridze (bl); Santiphoto (c). 22–23 Dreamstime.com: Qtrix. 23 Dreamstime.com: Mamuka Gotsiridze (bl). 24 Dreamstime.com:
Mamuka Gotsiridze (bl). 25 Dreamstime.com: Mamuka Gotsiridze (bl). 26 Alamy Images: Hirdes/F1online digitale Bildagentur GmbH (t). 26–27 Dreamstime.com:
Mike_kiev (b). 27 PunchStock: Blend Images. 28–29 123RF.com: federicofoto (t). 30 Dreamstime.com: Mike_kiev (b). 31 Dreamstime.com: Mamuka Gotsiridze (bl);
Nejron (c). 31 Dreamstime.com: Mamuka Gotsiridze (br); Nejron (c). 32–33 Dreamstime.com: Mike_kiev (b). 33 Dorling Kindersley: Bergen County, NJ, Law and
Public Safety Institute (t). 34 Corbis: Chris Carroll. 34–35 Dreamstime.com: Mike_kiev (b). 36 Dreamstime.com: Mamuka Gotsiridze (bl). Getty Images: Bloomberg
(crb). iStockphoto.com: hartphotography1 (cra). 37 Alamy Images: Victor Nikitin (crb). Dreamstime.com: Mamuka Gotsiridze (b). Getty Images: Glenn Asakawa
(cra). 38 Alamy Images: Hirdes/F1online digitale Bildagentur GmbH (t). iStockphoto.com: AlexSava (bc). 38–39 Dreamstime.com: Mike_kiev (b). 39 Corbis: Zero
Creatives (b). iStockphoto.com: one-image photography (b). 42–43 Dreamstime.com: Mike_kiev (b). 43 iStockphoto.com: AlexSava (bl). 44–45 123RF.com: Pat Olson (t). Dreamstime.com:
Mike_kiev (b). 45 iStockphoto.com: AlexSava (bc). 46 Alamy Images: Hirdes/F1online digitale Bildagentur GmbH (t). iStockphoto.com: franckreporter (b). 46–47
Dreamstime.com: Mike_kiev (b). 47 iStockphoto.com: gsmudger (t). 48 Alamy Images: FEMA (t). iStockphoto.com: franckreporter (br). 48–49 Dreamstime.com:
Mike_kiev (b). 50 Corbis: KIM KYUNG-HOON/Reuters (t). 50–51 Dreamstime.com: Mike_kiev (b). 51 iStockphoto.com: franckreporter (bl). 52–53 Dreamstime.
com: Mike_kiev (b). 52 iStockphoto.com: AlexSava (br); franckreporter (bc). 53 Alamy Images: Tom Grill/Corbis (c). Getty Images: Valerie Macon (br). 54
Dreamstime.com: Mike_kiev (b). 54–55 iStockphoto.com: Yuri_Arcurs (cra); Figure8Photos (clb). 55 Alamy Images: Picture Partners (tr). Dreamstime.com:
Mamuka Gotsiridze (br). 56–57 iStockphoto.com: t3000 (All Footprints). 56 Dreamstime.com: Mamuka Gotsiridze (bl). 57 Dreamstime.com: Mamuka Gotsiridze (br).
58 Getty Images: Valerie Macon (bc). 58–59 Dreamstime.com: Mike_kiev (b). 59 iStockphoto.com: AlexSava (br); franckreporter (br). 60–61 Dreamstime.com:
Mike_kiev (b). 60 Dreamstime.com: David Fowler (tr). Getty Images: Valerie Macon (bc). 61 iStockphoto.com: AlexSava (bl); franckreporter (br)
Jacket images: Front: Corbis: Darren Greenwood; Dorling Kindersley: Bergen County, NJ, Law and Public Safety Institute br, B&O Railroad Museum cr; Back:
Dreamstime.com: Fg76 l; iStockphoto.com: gsmudger r; Spine: PunchStock: Blend Images

All other images © Dorling Kindersley
For further information see: www.dkimages.com

A WORLD OF IDEAS:
SEE ALL THERE IS TO KNOW

www.dk.com

Contents

What's Your Emergency?

It's an **emergency**! Someone is in danger and needs urgent help. What should you do?

Call 9-1-1. This is the telephone number for the emergency services. Your call will be answered by an emergency **dispatcher**, whose job it is to tell police, fire, or medical services about emergencies.

A dispatcher will ask you what the emergency is and where it is happening. Emergency dispatchers need to be able to think quickly and stay calm. They are trained to handle lots of different situations and will help you with all kinds of emergencies.

If you call 9-1-1, you will be put through to an emergency call center. Sometimes, a computer can detect your **location**, but the dispatcher will always check your address anyway.

The dispatcher will take details of your emergency and contact your nearest police, fire department, or ambulance service. All of this happens in just a few minutes.

The dispatcher has contacted the fire department about an emergency. This firefighter is on the way.

Emergency dispatchers often stay
on the phone until help arrives. They
talk to callers to keep them calm. Most
importantly, they tell the caller what to
do until the emergency services arrive.

They can even tell callers
how to give first aid if someone
is choking or having a heart
attack. Emergency dispatchers
save many lives.

What to Do in an Emergency

Only call **9-1-1** if someone is hurt or in danger.

Call 9-1-1

- Say your name and where you are.

- Explain why you need help.

- Follow the dispatcher's instructions.

- Stay on the phone.

Remember:
try to stay calm.

If there's a fire

- Leave the building as quickly as you can.
- Crawl on the floor if there is smoke.
- Don't go back into the building.

If you need the police

- Go to a safe place right away.

If you need a doctor

- Don't move the person who is sick or hurt.

Be prepared for an **emergency**

- Memorize your parents' or caregivers' phone numbers.
- Post emergency numbers near the phone.
- Talk with your parents or caregivers about what to do in different emergencies.
- With your family, pick a safe place to go in case of emergencies, such as the house of a neighbor you trust.

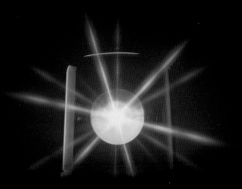

Chapter 1
POLICE

Help! Somebody broke into our house. Please come!

The police usually handle emergencies that involve crime. A crime is when someone breaks the law.

For example, a person breaking into someone else's house is a crime. People can help police stop crimes by reporting **suspicious** activity. This might include seeing a stranger go into a neighbor's house when no one's home or hearing someone scream. You should report suspicious activity by calling 9-1-1.

Police officers in the United Kingdom

The loud noise of a **siren** means the police are on their way to an emergency. The siren tells other drivers to get out of the way!

Police often wear **uniforms** so people know who they are. Sometimes they wear protective clothing as part of their uniform.

Police need special equipment to do their job. Most officers carry a weapon to defend themselves and a radio to speak to other police. They use handcuffs so suspected criminals can't get away.

The police handcuff a suspect to take to the police station.

Clues, such as fingerprints or traces of saliva, help **detectives** *solve a crime.*

Police do different jobs. For example, detectives **investigate** complicated crimes. Traffic police keep order on the roads. Specially trained police help in situations such as rescuing **hostages**.

Many police officers **patrol** neighborhoods to keep them safe. Some police drive patrol cars, while others ride on bicycles or horses, or even in boats or helicopters.

Police in Philadelphia, Pennsylvania

What does a police detective do?

If you want to be a police officer, you need to be physically fit and have lots of common sense. Police cadets train at a police academy. There, they learn about the law, first aid, and how to use police equipment.

Police cadets training in Mexico

They also need to do field training. This means teaming up with an experienced officer to get practice on the job. That way, they'll know what to do in different situations once they become police officers.

In Pursuit

Police use different ways of getting around, depending on where they are. It also depends whether they are on patrol or on their way to an emergency!

Helicopter, Spain

Jetski, Australia

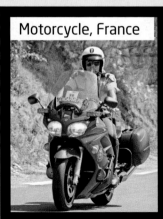

Motorcycle, France

Boat, Slovenia

Horse, Canada

Snowmobile, Germany

Bicycle, UK

Patrol car, US

21

Police Radio Codes

In some places, emergency dispatchers speak to the police on radios using special codes.

"51, a 211 at 2020 Sunset!"

This means: "Calling police officer with badge number 51. There's a robbery at the address 2020 Sunset Street."

Here are some radio codes used
by dispatchers and police officers:

Use these radio codes to
figure out what this means:

"A 925 in a 503. Code 2."

10-4	Ok
211	Robbery
503	Stolen vehicle
901	Traffic accident
901-N	Ambulance needed
904	Fire
925	Suspicious person
999	Officer needs help. EMERGENCY!

Code 1	Normal. Take this call next.
Code 2	Urgent! Hurry, but follow traffic laws. No red light or siren.
Code 3	Emergency! Use red light and siren.
Code 4	No further assistance needed.

Answer: A suspicious person in a stolen vehicle. Urgent! Hurry, but follow traffic laws. No red light or siren.

Fingerprints

Sometimes, criminals leave fingerprints behind. Everyone's fingerprints are unique, so they can be a useful clue in identifying a criminal.

A fingerprint kit might contain:

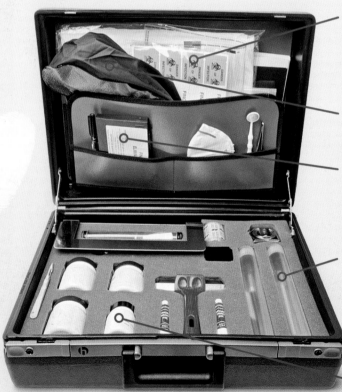

Evidence labels

Shoe covers

Fingerprint ink pad

Magnetic fingerprint brushes

Dusting powder

Step 1

Crime scientists use fine powder and a soft brush to gently dust the surface where fingerprints might be.

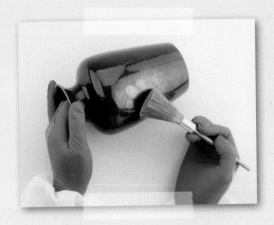

Step 2

They press clear tape on to the dusted print, and then peel it off so that the print comes with it.

Step 3

Fingerprints found at a crime scene are identified using a computerized system.

Chapter 2
FIRE

Help! My house is on fire!

Firefighters put out fires, rescue people from fires, and provide first aid to people in a fire situation. When they receive an emergency call, they zoom off in the fire truck as quickly as they can!

Firefighters often work for 24 hours at a time. They spend most of their days doing jobs around the fire station, exercising, training, and practicing a variety of **drills** for emergencies.

Sometimes they teach other people how to prevent fires. They might even come to your school!

A firefighter slides quickly down the fire pole on his way to an emergency.

Firefighters need to bring a lot of equipment on their trucks. This includes first aid supplies, ladders, **fire extinguishers**, and tools for breaking down doors or cutting cars open.

Fire trucks also carry about 1,000 feet (300 m) of hose. Firefighters pump water from the fire truck through the hose. Then they spray the water on the fire to put it out.

FIRE GEAR

Firefighters often have to get very close to fires, so their clothing and equipment protects them.

Helmet with visor protects head and eyes.

Hood protects neck.

Mask prevents breathing in smoke.

Coat, pants, and gloves resist heat and fire.

Firefighting gear weighs up to 75 lbs (34 kg).

Tank is filled with fresh air.

Radio used to speak to other firefighters.

Flashlight used for dark places.

Axes break down doors.

Boots with steel toes protect firefighters' feet.

Three things are needed for a fire: air, heat, and fuel. Paper, wood, and gasoline are some examples of fuel. To put out a fire, firefighters usually try to get rid of the air and heat by covering the fire with lots of water.

In a forest fire, firefighters often try
to remove the fuel, too. Trees are the fuel
in a forest fire. If firefighters destroy the
trees in the fire's path, there will be no
more trees for the fire to burn. That way,
they can save the rest of the forest.

This firefighter uses a special saw to free passengers trapped in a car accident.

Firefighters need to be strong and physically fit. They also have to be brave and able to stay calm under pressure.

Firefighters do lots of training. They learn about fire and how it can spread. They learn how to use firefighting and first aid equipment. They also learn about dangerous chemicals so they can make places safe after a chemical leak or spill. Firefighters practice rescuing people from car accidents, too.

Why do firefighters have to learn about dangerous chemicals?

Firefighter's Schedule

Firefighters work in shifts. There must be firefighters on duty day and night. They always need to be ready in case of an emergency!

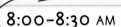 **8:00–8:30** AM

Check fire trucks are working and stocked with supplies.

8:30–9:00 AM

Meeting with the rest of the team.

9:00–12:30 AM

Training. This might be on firefighting techniques, first aid, or preventing fires.

12:00–1:00 PM

Lunch break. ....▼

1:00–3:00 PM

Jobs around the station. These might include cleaning the station or washing the trucks or equipment.

3:00–3:30 PM

Break.

3:30–5:00 PM

More jobs or training. ....

After 5:00 PM

Relax. Have dinner, read, or watch TV.

After 8:00 PM

Bedtime.

7:15 AM

Wake up and go home. The next shift reports for duty.

Chapter 3
AMBULANCE

Help! My husband's having a heart attack!

Emergency medical technicians, or EMTs, give emergency medical care. They are trained in first aid and other kinds of medical treatment. EMTs often drive to emergencies in ambulances, which have sirens just like police cars or fire trucks.

They help if someone has an accident or serious illness. For example, EMTs help if there is a car crash or if someone has a heart attack. EMTs provide quick medical care. They also take people to the hospital, where doctors can give patients further treatment.

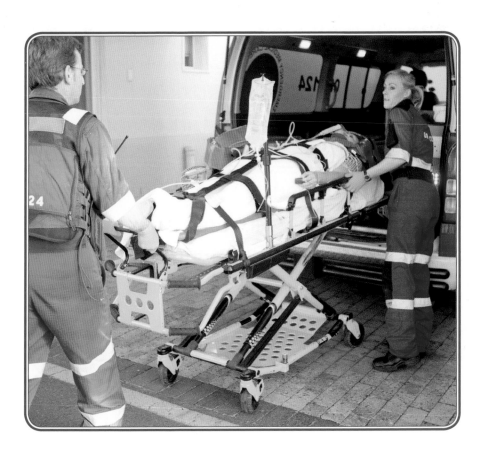

EMTs take lots of important equipment in the ambulance. Along with bandages and other basic first aid supplies, they take stretchers to carry patients.

They take oxygen tanks, masks, and other equipment to help people breathe. They take equipment for measuring heart rates and blood pressure, too.

They also take a defibrillator. This is a machine that uses electricity to help make someone's heart start beating again if it stops.

EMTs must wear gloves when treating people. This prevents passing **germs** between EMTs and patients.

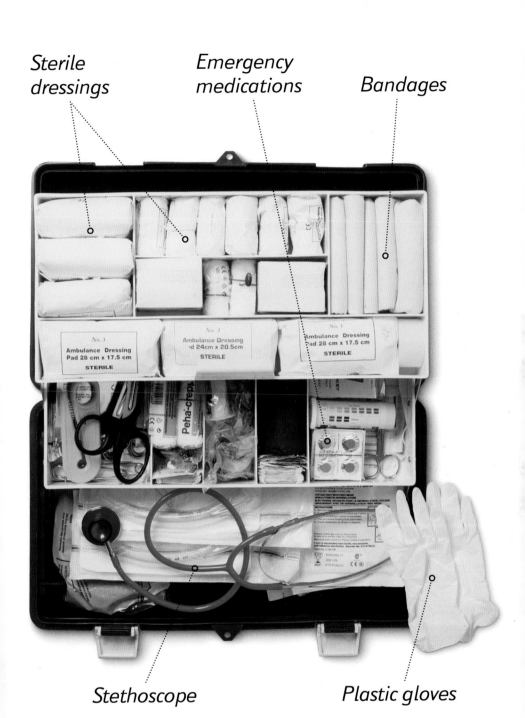

Sterile dressings

Emergency medications

Bandages

No. 3
Ambulance Dressing
Pad 28 cm x 17.5 cm
STERILE

No. 3
Ambulance Dressing
d 24cm x 20.5cm
STERILE

No. 3
Ambulance Dressing
Pad 28 cm x 17.5 cm
STERILE

Stethoscope

Plastic gloves

There are different levels of EMTs, depending on how much training they have had. Paramedics have the most training. They are allowed to give patients certain kinds of medicines as part of the emergency medical care.

Sometimes, police officers or firefighters are also trained as EMTs.

EMTs don't just travel in ambulances. They also travel in helicopters or on boats. EMTs might even travel on bicycles or snowmobiles. Any kind of transportation is used to save people's lives.

What is the EMT level with the most training called?

A motorcycle responder is often quicker and will give emergency care while waiting for an ambulance.

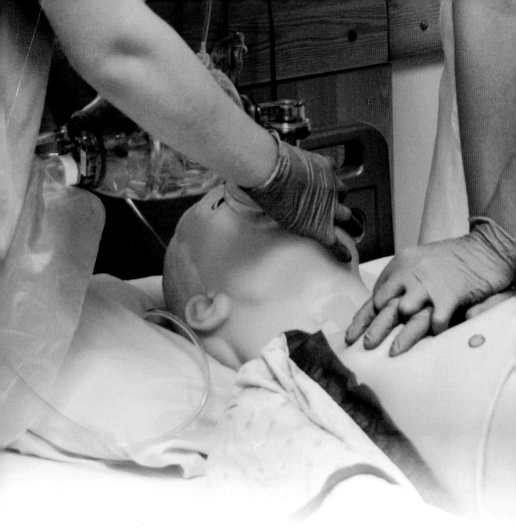

To be an EMT, you must be able to stay calm and make decisions quickly. You also need to be physically fit and strong enough to lift patients.

EMTs have special training to deal with medical emergencies. They learn

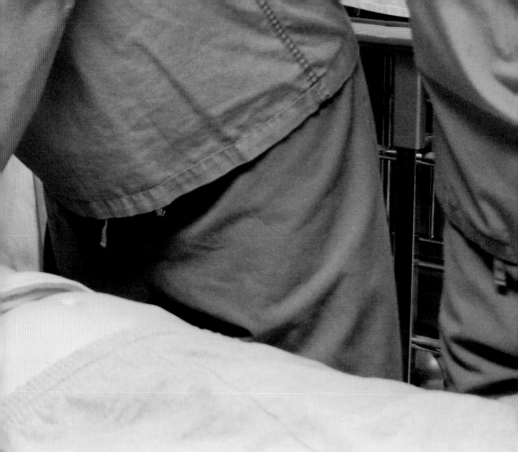

Practicing lifesaving on a mannequin.

lifesaving **techniques** to keep the blood and oxygen circulating around the body. They learn to monitor a patient's vital signs, including breathing and pulse. They also learn to put bandages on different types of wounds.

Chapter 4
SPECIAL
SERVICES

> *Help! I'm stuck on a mountain and I can't get back down....*

Sometimes other emergency services are needed, such as a search-and-rescue team. Their job is to find lost people and rescue them from dangerous situations.

A team member is lowered down to the rescue site.

Search-and-rescue teams find and rescue people from places that are hard to reach. These places include oceans, forests, mountains, deserts, caves, or mines. They often use helicopters to search from above. Once the rescue team locates the person who needs help, they may use other vehicles and equipment for the rescue.

A search-and-rescue team helps during a flood.

Search-and-rescue teams are not normally needed every day, so some teams are made up of **volunteers**. This means they give up their time to help others even though they don't get paid.

People who like adventure, especially in the wilderness, might want to join a search-and-rescue team. Like other emergency teams, they usually have special training. They learn how to use search-and-rescue equipment, plus first aid and survival skills.

Search-and-rescue teams are especially good at following tracks to find clues of people who are missing. Many are also good at other outdoor skills, such as sailing or climbing mountains.

Emergency relief workers in Japan make their way through heavy snow.

Emergency relief is a special service that brings food, water, and other urgent supplies to people affected by big emergencies. Disasters such as earthquakes, hurricanes, and blizzards are rare, but they can affect a lot of people across a wide area. Sometimes emergency relief teams drop supplies from planes or helicopters if they can't reach affected areas.

The Red Cross and Peace Corps provide this service around the world. They work with police, firefighters, EMTs, and search-and-rescue teams to help people survive disasters and get back to normal lives as quickly as possible.

Working for the emergency services may sound exciting, but it can be really scary, too. It's also hard work!

You can help the emergency services by talking to parents and teachers about how to stay safe and avoid emergencies.

Remember: don't call the emergency services unless there is an actual emergency. It will waste their time when they could be saving lives. Maybe one day you'll be the one saving lives!

How can you help the emergency services?

Rescue Animals

Animals are also used in the emergency services.

Dogs

Dogs have an incredible sense of smell. They can be trained by the police to find **illegal** things like drugs and bombs. These dogs form part of a K-9 unit.

Dogs are also extremely important to search-and-rescue teams and fire crews. They're very good at finding people. They can follow a trail with their noses, using the smell from a person's clothing.

Horses

Horses are used by both police and search-and-rescue teams. They can go places that cars cannot. Horses might even be trained to find people using their sense of smell.

Rats

Scientists hope that rats might also be trained to search for people in places that humans can't reach.

Cockroaches

In the future, search-and-rescue teams might even use cockroaches with mini-microphones attached to find people trapped in small spaces.

How to Follow Tracks

Here are some tips on how to find someone by following their tracks the way search-and-rescue teams do.

1 Find a track

Look at the ground to find a footprint. An area that is smoother or flatter than the ground around it might be a footprint.

2 Describe the track

Measure the length and width of the footprint with a ruler. Write down a description. Is the toe round or square? Does the sole have a pattern?

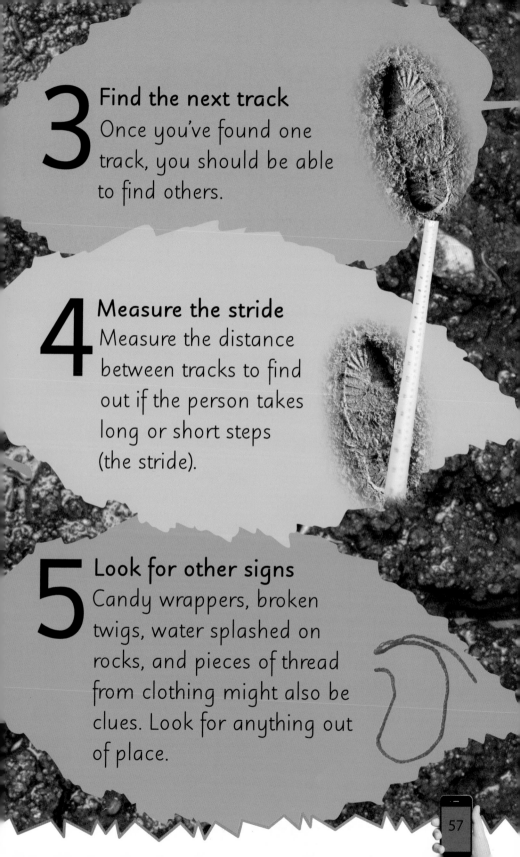

3 Find the next track

Once you've found one track, you should be able to find others.

4 Measure the stride

Measure the distance between tracks to find out if the person takes long or short steps (the stride).

5 Look for other signs

Candy wrappers, broken twigs, water splashed on rocks, and pieces of thread from clothing might also be clues. Look for anything out of place.

Emergency Quiz

Find the answers to these questions about what you have read. Answer correctly and help the ambulance get to the hospital.

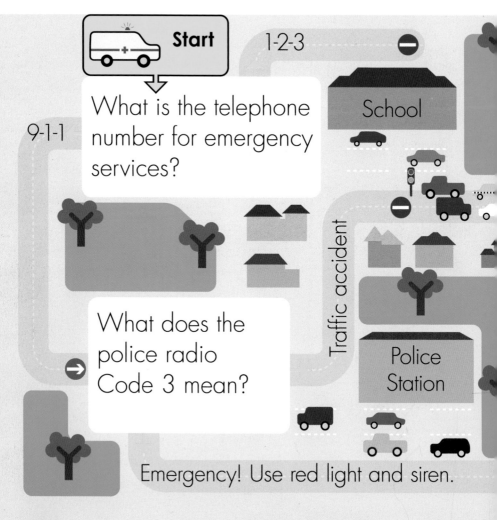

Start

1-2-3 ⛔

School

9-1-1

What is the telephone number for emergency services?

Traffic accident

Police Station

What does the police radio Code 3 mean?

Emergency! Use red light and siren.

58

What three things are needed for there to be a fire?

Fire Station

Air, heat, and fuel

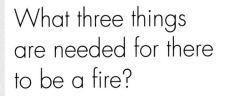

Water, heat, and fuel

Mall

How do search-and-rescue dogs follow a trail?

Lifesaving techniques

Using their sense of smell

Using their sense of touch

Finish Hospital

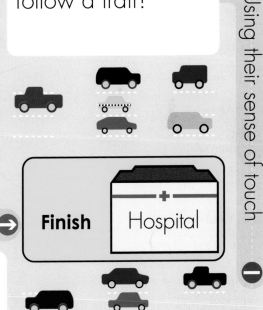

What kind of training do EMTs need?

Putting out a fire

Glossary

detective
police officer whose job is to investigate and solve crimes

dispatcher
someone who sends people where they are needed

drill
practice training

emergency
very serious and urgent situation

evidence
information gathered to prove that something is true

fire extinguisher
a container that releases a jet of water, foam, gas, or other material to put out a fire

first aid
immediate help for injury or illness

germs
tiny living things that can get into your body and make you sick

hostages
people being held against their will

illegal
forbidden by law

investigate
explore or research
to find answers

location
particular position
or place

patrol
keeping watch
over an area

siren
alarm that makes
a long, loud sound
to warn people

suspicious
appearing to
be doing
something wrong

technique
way of doing
something

uniform
clothing worn by
members of the
same group or
organization

volunteers
people who offer
their time to work
without being paid

Guide for Parents

DK Readers is a four-level interactive reading adventure series for children, developing the habit of reading widely for both pleasure and information. These books have an exciting main narrative interspersed with a range of reading genres to suit your child's reading ability. Each book is designed to develop your child's reading skills, fluency, grammar awareness, and comprehension in order to build confidence and engagement when reading.

Ready for a *Beginning to Read Alone* book

YOUR CHILD SHOULD

- be able to read many words without needing to stop and break them down into sound parts.
- read smoothly, in phrases and with expression.
  By this level, your child will be beginning to read silently.
- self-correct when a word or sentence doesn't sound right.

A VALUABLE AND SHARED READING EXPERIENCE

For some children, text reading, particularly non-fiction, requires much effort, but adult participation can make this both fun and easier. So here are a few tips on how to use this book with your child.

TIP 1 **Check out the contents together before your child begins:**

- invite your child to check the blurb, contents page, and layout of the book and comment on it.
- ask your child to make predictions about the story.
- talk about the information your child might want to find out.

TIP 2 **Encourage fluent and flexible reading:**

- support your child to read in fluent, expressive phrases, making full use of punctuation and thinking about the meaning.

- help your child learn to read with expression by choosing a sentence to read aloud and demonstrating how to do this.

TIP 3 Indicators that your child is reading for meaning:
- your child will be responding to the text if he/she is self-correcting and varying his/her voice.
- your child will want to talk about what he/she is reading or is eager to turn the page to find out what will happen next.

TIP 4 Chat at the end of each chapter:
- encourage your child to recall specific details after each chapter.
- let your child pick out interesting words and discuss what they mean.
- talk about what each of you found most interesting or most important.
- ask questions about the text. These help to develop comprehension skills and awareness of the language used.

A FEW ADDITIONAL TIPS
- Read to your child regularly to demonstrate fluency, phrasing, and expression; to find out or check information; and for sharing enjoyment.
- Encourage your child to reread favorite texts to increase reading confidence and fluency.
- Check that your child is reading a range of different types of material, such as poems, jokes, and following instructions.

Series consultant, **Dr. Linda Gambrell**, Distinguished Professor of Education at Clemson University, has served as President of the National Reading Conference, the College Reading Association, and the International Reading Association.

Index